Rotten Logs and Forest Floors

Sharon Katz Cooper

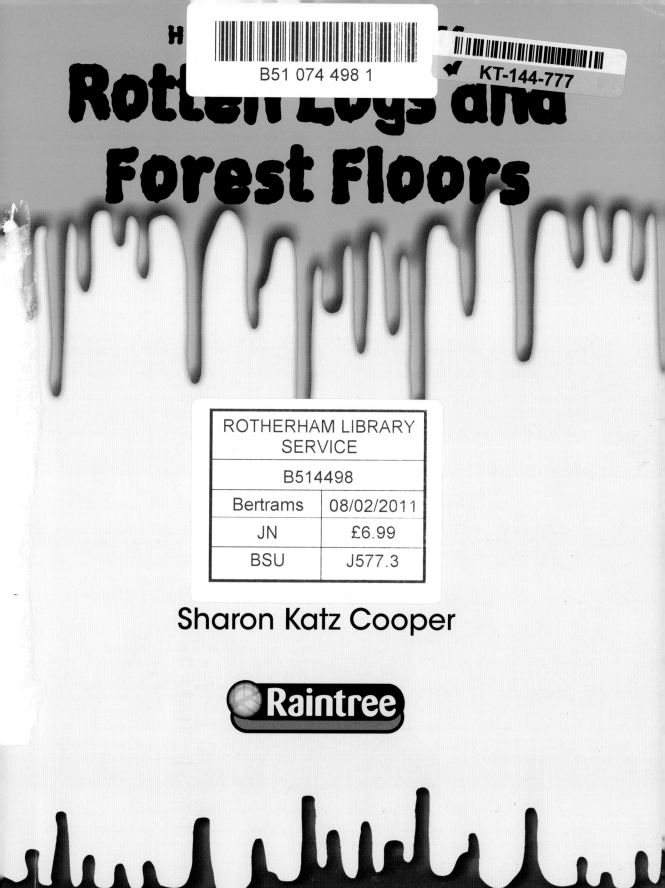

Raintree

www.raintreepublishers.co.uk
Visit our website to find out
more information about
Raintree books.

To order:
☎ Phone 0845 6044371
📄 Fax +44 (0) 1865 312263
📧 Email myorders@raintreepublishers.co.uk

Customers from outside the UK please telephone +44 1865 312262

Raintree is an imprint of Capstone Global Library Limited, a
company incorporated in England and Wales having its registered
office at 7 Pilgrim Street, London, EC4V 6LB – Registered
company number: 6695582

Edited by Charlotte Guillain, Rebecca Rissman,
and Siân Smith
Designed by Joanna Hinton-Malivoire
Picture research by Tracy Cummins and Heather Mauldin
Originated by Chroma Graphics (Overseas) Pte. Ltd
Printed and bound in China by Leo Paper Products

ISBN 978 1 406212 91 4 (hardback)
14 13 12 11 10
10 9 8 7 6 5 4 3 2 1

ISBN 978 1 406212 99 0 (paperback)
14 13 12 11 10
10 9 8 7 6 5 4 3 2 1

British Library Cataloguing in Publication Data
Katz Cooper, Sharon.
Rotten logs and forest floors. -- (Horrible habitats)
577.3-dc22
A full catalogue record for this book is available from the British
Library.

Acknowledgements
The author and publisher are grateful to the following for
permission to reproduce copyright material:
Age Fotostock p. **10** (© Joel Sartore); Alamy pp. **6**
(© Chuck Place), **17** (© Scott Camazine), **20** (© Arco
Images/Muehlmann, K.), **22** (© Nature Picture Library/Jose
B. Ruiz), **23** (© Bruce Coleman Inc./John Bell); Bugwood.org
p. **26** (© Scott Bauer, USDA Agricultural Research Service);
Dwight Kuhn Photography p. **19** (© Dwight Kuhn); Getty
Images p. **12** (© Bill Beatty); Minden p. **11** (© Mark Moffett);
Nature Picture Library p. **14** (© Adrian Davies); Photolibrary
pp. **8** (© Science Photo Library), **18** (© Oxford Scientific), **25**
(© Michael Fogden); Shutterstock pp. **4** (© Kirsanov), **5** (©
letty17), **7** (© Aleksander Bolbot), **9**, **13** (© Joseph Calev), **15**
(© Neale Cousland), **21** (© Gert Johannes Jacobus Vrey), **29**
background (© Vojta Herout), **29a** (© Nicholas Piccillo), **29b**
(© Graham Taylor), **29c** (© Pakhnyushcha), **29d** (© Babusi
Octavian Florentin), **29e** (© Ljupco Smokovski), **29f** (©
pixelman); Visuals Unlimited, Inc. pp. **16** (© Steve Strickland),
24 (© Dr. Dennis Kunkel), **27** (© Dr. Dennis Kunkel).

Cover photograph of an earthworm reproduced
with permission of Photo Researchers, Inc. (© Wayne
G. Lawler).

Every effort has been made to contact copyright holders
of material reproduced in this book. Any omissions will
be rectified in subsequent printings if notice is given
to the publishers.

Some words are shown in bold, **like this**. You can find
out what they mean by looking in the glossary.

Contents

What is a habitat?

A **habitat** is a place where animals can get the things they need to live. Just like you, they need food, water, and shelter.

frog

newly fallen tree

6

rotting tree

Can you spot the differences between this rotting tree and the tree that has just fallen?

A tree falls in the forest. Crash! But that is not the end of the tree's story. It's just the beginning of its new life as a rotting **habitat**.

Who's on your back?

Rotting logs are full of creatures so tiny you can't see them. These are called **microbes**. They often ride into the log on an ant's body.

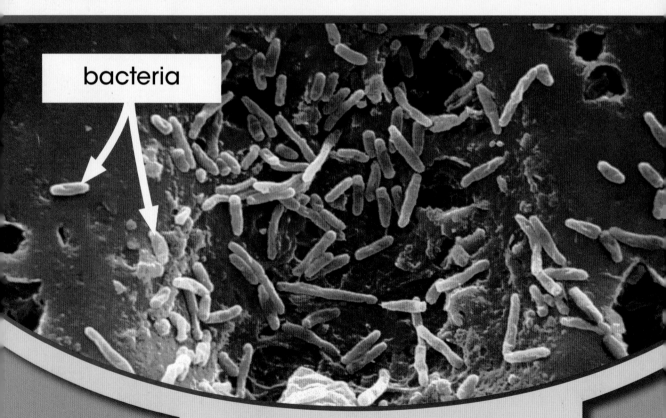

bacteria

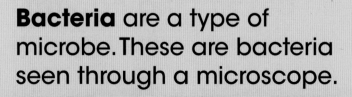

Bacteria are a type of microbe. These are bacteria seen through a microscope.

Bacteria living on ants make **antibiotics**. These antibiotics help stop ants and their babies getting ill.

9

Slurp and burp!

Bess beetles use **microbes** in their guts to **digest**, or break down, rotting wood. Baby beetles do not have these microbes. To get them, they call to an adult beetle. The adult beetle vomits food with microbes into the baby's mouth.

larva

adult beetle

This photo shows adult beetles and a baby beetle, or **larva**.

Have you ever seen a woodlouse? They like to eat anything that is rotting. On the forest floor, they eat rotting leaves and wood.

woodlouse

FUN FACT

Woodlice are not insects. They are related to lobsters and crabs!

new shell

old shell

As woodlice grow, they lose their old shells and grow new ones. This is called **moulting**.

13

Once a log gets soft from holes and water, new creatures come to eat. They come to eat the wood-eaters and their poo. Some even eat the **microbes** growing on poo. Yum!

soft, wet wood

fungus

Some insects plant a **fungus** garden on their log. Fungus is like mould or mushrooms. The insects plant a tiny bit of fungus on the log. When the fungus grows, they eat it!

Here come the ants!

Some ants love rotting logs. They don't eat wood. They dig through it to make a shelter. Inside a log, rain and wind can't bother them!

eggs

FUN FACT

The carpenter ant queen lays many eggs. When the first ones hatch into babies or **larvae**, she feeds her other eggs to them.

Welcome worms

Earthworms squirm through rotting logs and forest floors to eat their favourite foods. They chomp on poo and pieces of dead plants and animals.

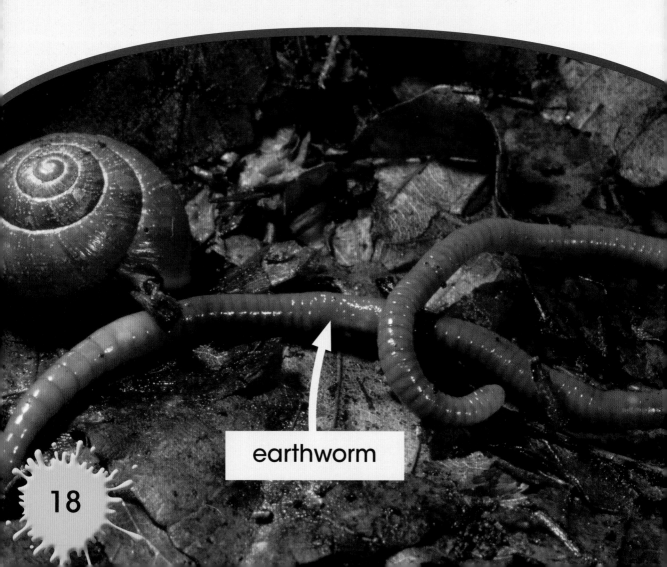

earthworm

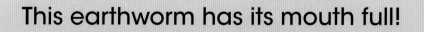

leaf

This earthworm has its mouth full!

Feasting on poo

Millipedes chew up dead leaves and wood and leave their poo behind. **Microbes** grow on that poo. Those microbes make a very tasty feast for creatures like springtails and mites!

springtail

millipede

Blind and dangerous

The forest floor is home to many centipedes. Most are blind. But watch out! They are dangerous killers. They kill insects for food by **injecting**, or putting, poison into them.

This centipede is busy eating a spider.

Battling termites

There can be many termites in a rotting log. Soldier termites protect their **colony**, or group, from enemies like ants. Some soldier termites have no eyes. Instead, they have giant heads and long, sharp jaws.

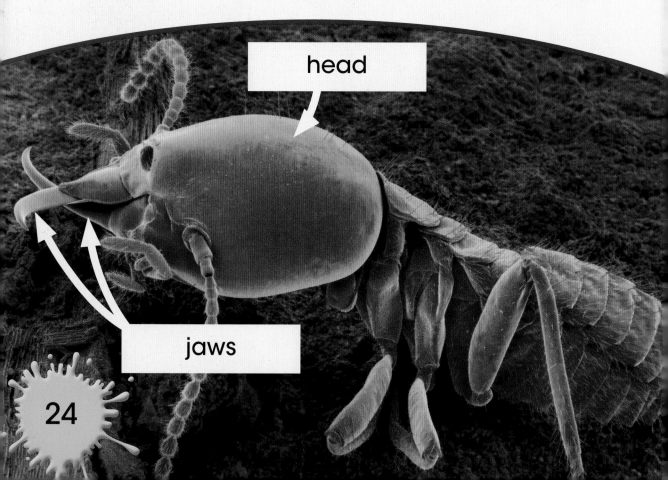

head

jaws

24

Soldier termites can be male or female.

FUN FACT

If the **colony** runs low on food, the worker termites eat the soldier termites. They don't fight back – they just give themselves up as lunch!

Some soldier termites protect the colony in another way. They shoot out poison goo from their foreheads.

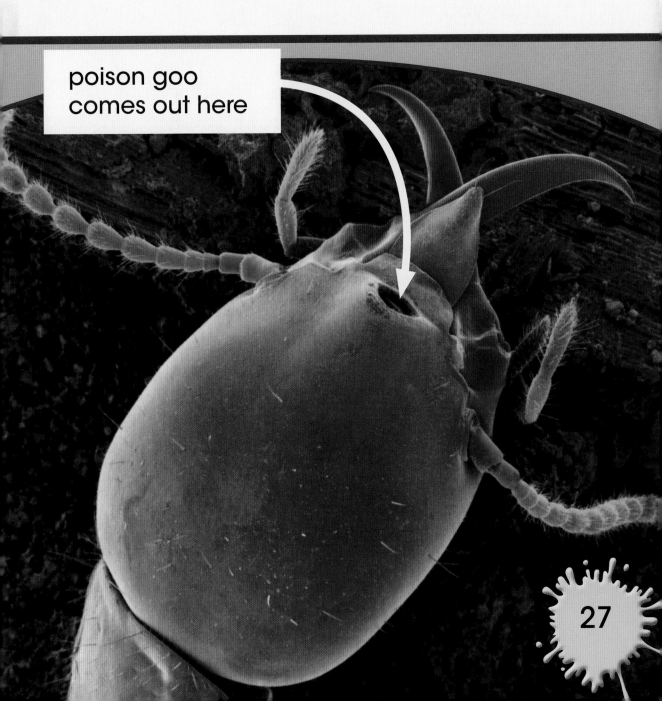

poison goo comes out here

Explore a rotting tree

What you need:
- magnifying glass
- your eyes

What to do:
1. Find a rotting log in a nearby forest or park.

2. Look around carefully. See how many of these things you can find:

a. an earthworm
b. a beetle
c. an ant
d. a millipede
e. a mushroom
f. a woodlouse

Glossary

antibiotic substance, like a medicine, that is used to stop illnesses caused by living things such as bacteria or fungus

bacteria type of microbe. Some bacteria can cause illness in people and other animals.

colony large group of animals

digest to break down food inside the body so that it can be used

fungus plant-like living things, similar to mushrooms

habitat place where animals or plants live and grow

inject to put something into something else

larvae the young of some types of insects

microbe tiny living thing that can only be seen under a microscope

moulting when an animal sheds its skin or shell and grows a new one

Find out more

Find out

How do ants hear without ears?

Books to read

Bug Books: Woodlouse, Stephanie St. Pierre (Heinemann Library, 2008)

Habitat Explorer: Forest Explorer, Greg Pyers (Raintree, 2004)

The Amazing World of Microlife: Microlife that Rots Things, Steve Parker (Raintree, 2006)

Websites

http://www.earthlife.net/insects/ants.html
This website gives you lots of information about ants.

http://www.enchantedlearning.com/biomes/
This website gives you illustrations of many forest animals.

http://www.pestworldforkids.org/ants.html
This website has lots of fascinating facts about ants.

Index